1104429

Earthforms

Canyons

by Christine Webster

Consultant:
Robert S. Anderson, PhD
Associate Professor of Geological Sciences
University of Colorado at Boulder

Capstone *press*

Mankato, Minnesota

Bridgestone Books are published by Capstone Press,
151 Good Counsel Drive, P.O. Box 669, Mankato, Minnesota 56002.
www.capstonepress.com

Library of Congress Cataloging-in-Publication Data
Webster, Christine.
    Canyons / by Christine Webster.
       p. cm.—(Bridgestone books. Earthforms)
    Includes bibliographical references and index.
    ISBN 0-7368-3711-6 (hardcover)
    1. Canyons—Juvenile literature. I. Title. II. Series.
GB562.W385 2005
551.4'42—dc22   2004014275

Summary: Describes canyons, including how they form, plants and animals in canyons, how people and
    weather change canyons, canyons in North America, and canyons of the world.

Editorial Credits

Becky Viaene, editor; Juliette Peters, designer; Anne McMullen, illustrator; Wanda Winch,
    photo researcher; Scott Thoms, photo editor

Photo Credits

Corbis/Royalty-Free, 16; William Manning, cover
Corel, 1, 14
James P. Rowan, 4, 6
Nature Picture Library/Huw Cordey, 10
OneBlueShoe, 12
Steve Mulligan, 8
Sunracer Photography and Publishers/Richard D. Fisher, 18

1 2 3 4 5 6 10 09 08 07 06 05

Table of Contents

What Are Canyons?

Canyons are like valleys. Both have low land between two areas of higher land. Usually a river flows through them. Valleys are found between two hills or mountains. Canyons are found between two cliffs.

Rivers carve canyons out of rock. Canyons have very steep sides. Some canyon walls are almost straight up and down.

◄ Cut by the Hvita River in Iceland, the steep walls of this canyon rise almost 230 feet (70 meters).

How Do Canyons Form?

Rivers wear away rock to form canyons. Water in rivers flows quickly through a **channel**.

The water carries small rocks and sand, called **sediment**. The sediment cuts into rocks near the channel, wearing them down. This action is called **erosion**. Rivers can take millions of years to cut deep channels into rocks.

◄ Utah's San Juan River cut through these rocks. Steep, curving canyons like this one are called goosenecks.

Plants in Canyons

Steep canyon walls have little dirt to hold plant roots. Still, some mosses can grow on rocky canyon walls. Mosses do not need dirt to grow.

Other plants grow on canyon floors near rivers. Grasses, trees, and wildflowers are found on canyon floors. Cactuses grow on dry canyon floors. Some of these plants are food for animals living in canyons.

◄ Plants grow on the canyon floor near the San Juan River in Utah.

Animals in Canyons

Canyon walls are home to many birds. Birds live in canyon walls. Owls, hawks, and eagles build their nests there. Rock wrens also live in canyon walls. These birds are all found in Arizona's Grand Canyon. Birds fly down to canyon floors. They look for food and water there.

Animals also live on canyon floors and in canyon rivers. Lizards and snakes live on some canyon floors. Fish swim in canyon rivers. Turtles live near canyon rivers.

◄ A chuckwalla lizard suns itself on a rock. These lizards search canyon floors for plants to eat.

Weather Changes Canyons

Over time, wet weather can change canyons. Rain and melting snow add water to rivers. The rivers flow faster. Fast-moving water erodes river bottoms more quickly. The canyons get deeper.

Cold weather also changes canyons. Water flows into cracks in canyon rocks. Cold weather makes the water freeze. Water expands when it freezes. Ice pushes against rocks. It can break off pieces of rock.

◄ Ice from a frozen waterfall can break up rocks, causing them to fall to the canyon floor.

People Change Canyons

People sometimes build walls called **dams** across canyons. Dams make electricity and provide water for crops.

Dams change canyons. They stop rivers from flowing naturally. The water behind a dam creates a lake. Most sediment stays in the lake and can't erode canyon walls.

Dams can change canyons' plant and animal life. Some plants and animals in canyons can't live by dams. Dams often block fish from swimming and finding food.

◄ Arizona's Glen Canyon Dam provides electricity for five states. Lake Powell is behind the dam.

Canyons in North America

North America has more than 1,000 canyons. The largest canyon in the United States is Arizona's Grand Canyon. The Grand Canyon is 277 miles (446 kilometers) long. It is about 6,000 feet (1,800 meters) deep.

The deepest canyon in North America is called Hells Canyon. It is on the border between Oregon and Idaho. Hells Canyon is more than 8,000 feet (2,400 meters) deep.

◄ The Grand Canyon's floor can be 25 degrees Fahrenheit (14 degrees Celsius) hotter than its top.

Canyons of the World

Amazing canyons are found all over the world. One of the world's deepest is Peru's Colca Canyon. It is twice as deep as the Grand Canyon.

Length and depth are used to decide which canyon is the world's largest. The largest canyon in world is the Yarlung Zangbo in China. The canyon is 17,657 feet (5,382 meters) deep and 308 miles (496 kilometers) long.

◀ The Zangbo River flows through the Yarlung Zangbo Canyon in Tibet, China.

The Grand Canyon

Colorado River

N
W · E
S

LEGEND

Feet		Meters
12,000		4,000
9,000		3,000
6,000		2,000
4,500		1,500
3,000		1,000
1,200		400
600		200
0		0

ARIZONA

Canyons on a Map

Canyons can be seen on **elevation** maps. On these maps, different colors show different elevations. Often, blue lines show rivers running through canyons.

On a map, the power of rivers running through canyons isn't shown. But powerful rivers have changed canyons' pasts and will continue to shape their futures.

◄ On this map, the Grand Canyon is a light-colored, narrow area, surrounded by darker colors.

Glossary

channel (CHAN-uhl)—a narrow stretch of water between two areas of land

dam (DAM)—a wall built across a river or stream to hold back water

elevation (el-uh-VAY-shuhn)—the height above sea level; sea level is defined as zero elevation.

erosion (i-ROH-zhuhn)—a slow wearing away of soil and rock by water and wind

sediment (SED-uh-muhnt)—rocks, sand, or dirt carried to a place by water, wind, or a glacier

Read More

Brimner, Larry Dane. *Valleys and Canyons.* A True Book. New York: Children's Press, 2000.

Kallen, Stuart A. *The Grand Canyon.* Wonders of the World. San Diego: Kidhaven Press, 2003.

Internet Sites

FactHound offers a safe, fun way to find Internet sites related to this book. All of the sites on FactHound have been researched by our staff.

Here's how:
1. Visit *www.facthound.com*
2. Type in this special code **0736837116** for age-appropriate sites. Or enter a search word related to this book for a more general search.
3. Click on the **Fetch It** button.

FactHound will fetch the best sites for you!

Index